JAN'S KWAJALEIN ADVENTURES

REMEMBERING NEW MEXICO

Anake Kanike

AuthorHouse™
1663 Liberty Drive
Bloomington, IN 47403
www.authorhouse.com
Phone: 833-262-8899

Because of the dynamic nature of the Internet, any web addresses or links contained in this book may have changed since publication and may no longer be valid. The views expressed in this work are solely those of the author and do not necessarily reflect the views of the publisher, and the publisher hereby disclaims any responsibility for them.

Any people depicted in stock imagery provided by Getty Images are models, and such images are being used for illustrative purposes only.
Certain stock imagery © Getty Images.

This book is printed on acid-free paper.

ISBN: 978-1-6655-2806-1 (sc)
ISBN: 978-1-6655-2808-5 (hc)
ISBN: 978-1-6655-2807-8 (e)

Print information available on the last page.

Published by AuthorHouse 07/27/2021

authorHOUSE®

JAN'S KWAJALEIN
ADVENTURES
REMEMBERING NEW MEXICO

Dedication

This book is dedicated to my father and mother, for without them this book would not be; for not only would I have not been born, but my early childhood years would never have been graced by the wondrous beauty of Kwajalein life.

Hello! My name is Jan. I am three years old. I was born in Oklahoma.

This is Dad and Mom. They met in one of their college classes. They were going to college to become Electrical Engineers.

After I turned two, my parents and I moved to Las Cruces, New Mexico.

This is a picture of our home where we live.

We moved to Las Cruses so Dad could work out at White Sands.

It is called White Sands because the sands are so white.

White Sands is where they work on missiles for our national defense.

WHITE SANDS MISSILE RANGE
A TESTING GROUND FOR
GUIDED MISSILE PROGRAMS
OF THE
ARMY - NAVY - AIR FORCE

Dad designs radar guidance for Nike missiles. We have been living here in New Mexico for about a year.

However, today is moving day. Yes, I am only three and we are moving to a third home. Our new home is a teeny tiny island in the middle of the Pacific Ocean just north of the equator. The name of this island is Kwajalein. Mom and Dad call it Kwaj. I am so excited! I can hardly wait to see our new home.

Now I do not know about you, but I do not know what an ocean is. I asked Mom what an ocean is. She said it is a giant body of water.

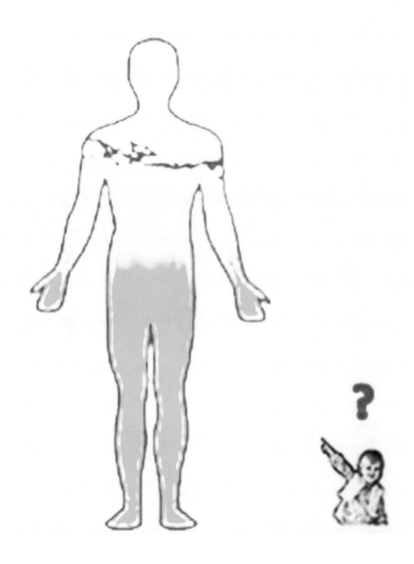

Later, she went on to mention that people swim in the ocean. Playing in the water was my very first memory. I thought it was simply divine!

Mom also told me that fish and other sea animals live in the ocean, animals like the:

Sea Turtle

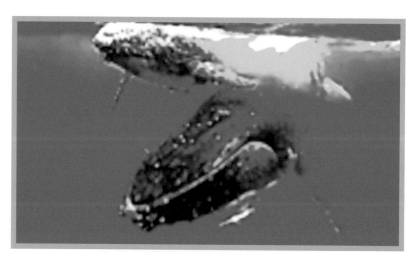

Humpback Whale

Dolphin

Seahorse

Octopus

Starfish

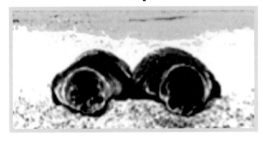

Monk Seal

and

Clown Fish

I love animals. This ocean thing sounded better and better.

Mom and Dad have been packing for days.

Plus, Mom said the worst part was over!

Just trust me when I say no kid wants to go through what I had to go through!

Anytime an American is going to leave the United States and go to a different place in the world, that person may have to get many shots to be protected from diseases so they don't get sick. But boy do those shots really, really hurt!

The nurse gave me a cherry lollipop and it did taste awesome, but I still cried all the way home.

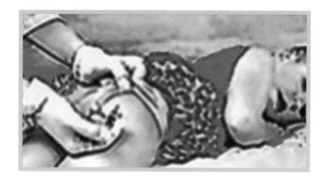

They hurt so bad that I could not sit down for hours!

We also needed a small book called a passport. It had our picture in it. Well, Dad had his own. Mom and I shared one as our picture was taken with me sitting on Mom's lap.

A passport is like a movie ticket. When someone goes to see a movie, that person must show the movie ticket before getting in to see the movie.

With the passport, we can go to the country we are moving to, and return to the United States of America. Thank goodness, those requirements are done.

I am excited to see our new home, but I am going to miss New Mexico. So far, I have some exciting memories of our living in New Mexico.

I remember going to White Sands and climbing up the sand dunes and sliding down them.

On our road trips, we saw many fun things.

One time, we got to see a real mountain lion.

Mom and Dad also love to camp. We go camping at national forests and state parks here in New Mexico.

Some of my favorite memories are when we camped near Cloudcroft.

I also loved camping near ancient Pueblo Indian homes.

Pueblo means a village. Different Indian tribes make up the Pueblo Indians.

The oldest tribes were hunters and are called the Sandia tribe and Clovis tribe. These are Clovis spearheads.

After those two tribes, the Cochise Tribe appeared. They were hunters, but the Cochise also knew how to gather and grow crops of grain.

The Anasazi Tribe came after the Cochise Tribe. The Anasazi were excellent basket weavers and pottery makers.

They also loved vibrant colors that they used when making their ceremonial clothes.

In addition to seeing some of their homes, we also got to see some of their picture-art they drew on the cave and cliff walls, called Petroglyphs.

Another camping road trip took us to Carlsbad Caverns.

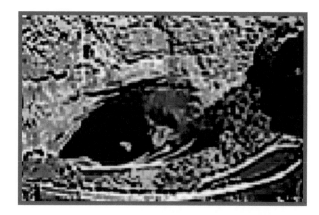

We got to walk down inside along a pathway.

 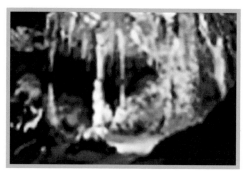 

It has many unusual sculptures inside.

Carlsbad Caverns is also the home for a giant group of bats. During the day they sleep inside the cave.

But at night, they come out to hunt for food and to play bat games. In the evening, visitors can sit in an area to watch the bats fly out of the mouth of the cave into the darkening sky.

Yes, our road and camping trips were lots of fun! I am going to miss them.

I wonder if we will go on trips on Kwajalein. In just a few more days, I will be on Kwaj and then I will see just what fun Kwaj will offer!

JOIN JAN ON HER NEXT ADVENTURE
TRIP TO EL PASO

Printed in the United States
by Baker & Taylor Publisher Services